The Epistle of Mathetes to Diognetus

Copyright © 2016 Beloved Publishing

All rights reserved. No part of this book may be reproduced, scanned, or distributed in any printed or electronic form without permission.

Beloved Publishing

Pickerington, Ohio

www.BelovedPublishing.com - "Discover a Classic"

Printed in the United States of America

First edition

ISBN:1631741373

The Epistle of Mathetes to Diognetus

Introductory Note to the Epistle of Mathetes to Diognetus

[a.d. 130.] The anonymous author of this Epistle gives himself the title (Mathetes) "a disciple of the Apostles," and I venture to adopt it as his name. It is about all we know of him, and it serves a useful end. I place his letter here, as a sequel to the Clementine Epistle, for several reasons, which I think scholars will approve: (1) It is full of the Pauline spirit, and exhales the same pure and primitive fragrance which is characteristic of Clement. (2) No theory as to its date very much conflicts with that which I adopt, and it is sustained by good authorities. (3) But, as a specimen of the persuasives against Gentilism which early Christians employed in their intercourse with friends who adhered to heathenism, it admir- ably illustrates the temper prescribed by St. Paul (2 Tim. ii. 24), and not less the peculiar social relations of converts to the Gospel with the more amiable and candid of their personal friends at this early period.

Mathetes was possibly a catechumen of St. Paul or of one of the apostle's associates. I assume that his correspondent was the tutor of M. Aurelius. Placed just here, it fills a lacuna in the series, and takes the place of the pseudo (second) Epistle of Clement, which is now relegated to its proper place with the works falsely ascribed to St. Clement.

The Epistle of Mathetes to Diognetus

Altogether, the Epistle is a gem of purest ray; and, while suggesting some difficulties as to interpretation and exposition, it is practically clear as to argument and intent. Mathetes is, perhaps, the first of the apologists.

The following is the original Introductory Notice of the learned editors and translators:—

The following interesting and eloquent Epistle is anonymous, and we have no clue whatever as to its author. For a considerable period after its publication in 1592, it was generally ascribed to Justin Martyr. In recent times Otto has inserted it among the works of that writer, but Semisch and others contend that it cannot possibly be his. In dealing with this question, we depend entirely upon the internal evidence, no statement as to the author- ship of the Epistle having descended to us from antiquity. And it can scarcely be denied that the whole tone of the Epistle, as well as special passages which it contains, points to some other writer than Justin. Accordingly, critics are now for the most part agreed that it is not his, and that it must be ascribed to one who lived at a still earlier date in the history of the Church. Several internal arguments have been brought forward in favour of this opinion. Supposing chap. xi. to be genuine, it has been supported by the fact that the writer there styles himself "a disciple of the apostles." But there is great suspicion that the two concluding chapters are spurious; and even though admitted to be genuine, the expression quoted evidently admits of a different explanation from that which implies the writer's personal acquaintance with the apostles: it might, indeed, be adopted by one even at the present day. More weight is to be attached to those passages in which the writer speaks of Christianity as still being a new thing in the world. Expressions to this effect occur in several places (chap. i., ii., ix.), and seem to imply that the author lived very little, if at all, after the apostolic age. There is certainly nothing in the Epistle which is inconsistent with this opinion; and we may therefore believe, that in this beautiful composition we possess a genuine production of some apostolic man who lived not later than the beginning of the second century.

The names of Clement of Rome and of Apollos have both been suggested as those of the probable author. Such opinions, however, are pure fancies, which it is perhaps impossible to refute, but which rest on nothing more than conjecture. Nor can a single word be said as to the person named Diognetus, to whom the letter is addressed. We must be content to leave both points in hopeless obscurity, and simply accept the Epistle as written by an earnest and intelligent Christian to a sincere inquirer among the Gentiles, towards the close of the apostolic age.

The Epistle of Mathetes to Diognetus

It is much to be regretted that the text is often so very doubtful. Only three mss. of the Epistle, all probably exhibiting the same original text, are known to exist; and in not a few passages the readings are, in consequence, very defective and obscure. But notwithstanding this drawback, and the difficulty of representing the full force and elegance of the original, this Epistle, as now presented to the English reader, can hardly fail to excite both his deepest interest and admiration.

[N.B.—Interesting speculations concerning this precious work may be seen in Bunsen's Hippolytus and his Age, vol. i. p. 188. The learned do not seem convinced by this author, but I have adopted his suggestion as to Diognetus the tutor of M. Aurelius.]

The Epistle of Mathetes to Diognetus

The Epistle of Mathetes to Diognetus

Chapter I.—Occasion of the epistle.

Since I see thee, most excellent Diognetus, exceedingly desirous to learn the mode of worshipping God prevalent among the Christians, and inquiring very carefully and earnestly concerning them, what God they trust in, and what form of religion they observe, so as all to look down upon the world itself, and despise death, while they neither esteem those to be gods that are reckoned such by the Greeks, nor hold to the superstition of the Jews; and what is the affection which they cherish among themselves; and why, in fine, this new kind or practice [of piety] has only now entered into the world, and not long ago; I cordially welcome this thy desire, and I implore God, who enables us both to speak and to hear, to grant to me so to speak, that, above all, I may hear you have been edified, and to you so to hear, that I who speak may have no cause of regret for having done so.

Chapter II.—The vanity of idols.

Come, then, after you have freed yourself from all prejudices possessing your mind, and laid aside what you have been accustomed to, as something apt to deceive you, and being made, as if from the beginning, a new man, inasmuch as, according to your own confession, you are to be the hearer of a new [system of] doctrine; come and contemplate, not with your eyes only, but with your understanding, the substance and the form of those whom ye declare and deem to be gods. Is not one of them a stone similar to that on which we tread? Is not a second brass, in no way superior to those vessels which are constructed for our ordinary use? Is not a third wood, and that already rotten? Is not a fourth silver, which needs a man to watch it, lest it be stolen? Is not a fifth iron, consumed by rust? Is not a sixth earthenware, in no degree more valuable than that which is formed for the humblest purposes? Are not all these of corruptible matter? Are they not fabricated by means of iron and fire? Did not the sculptor fashion one of them, the brazier a second, the silversmith a third, and the potter a fourth? Was not every one of them, before they were formed by the arts of these [workmen] into the shape of these [gods], each in its own way subject to change? Would not those things which are now vessels, formed of the same materials, become like to such, if they met with the same artificers? Might not these, which are now worshipped by you, again be made by men vessels similar to others? Are they not all deaf? Are they not blind? Are they not without life? Are they not destitute of feeling? Are they not incapable of motion? Are they not all liable to rot? Are they not all corruptible? These things ye call gods; these ye serve; these ye worship; and ye become altogether like to them. For this reason ye hate the Christians, because they do not deem these to be gods. But do not ye yourselves, who now think and suppose [such to be gods], much more cast contempt upon them than they [the Christians do]? Do ye not much more mock and insult them, when ye worship those that are made of stone and earthenware, without appointing any persons to guard them; but those made of silver and gold ye shut up by night, and appoint watchers to look after them by day, lest they be stolen? And by those gifts which ye mean to present to them, do ye not, if they are possessed of sense, rather punish [than honour] them? But if, on the other hand, they are destitute of sense, ye convict them of this fact, while ye worship them with blood and the smoke of sacrifices. Let any one of you suffer such indignities! Let any one of you endure to have such things done to himself! But not a single human being will, unless compelled to it, endure such treatment, since he is endowed with sense and reason. A stone, however, readily bears it, seeing it is insensible. Certainly you do not show [by your conduct] that he [your God] is possessed of sense. And as to the fact that Christians are not accustomed to serve such gods, I might easily find many other things to say; but if even what has been said does not seem to any one sufficient, I deem it idle to say anything further.

Chapter III.—Superstitions of the Jews.

And next, I imagine that you are most desirous of hearing something on this point, that the Christians do not observe the same forms of divine worship as do the Jews. The Jews, then, if they abstain from the kind of service above described, and deem it proper to worship one God as being Lord of all, [are right]; but if they offer Him worship in the way which we have described, they greatly err. For while the Gentiles, by offering such things to those that are destitute of sense and hearing, furnish an example of madness; they, on the other hand, by thinking to offer these things to God as if He needed them, might justly reckon it rather an act of folly than of divine worship. For He that made heaven and earth, and all that is therein, and gives to us all the things of which we stand in need, certainly requires none of those things which He Himself bestows on such as think of furnishing them to Him. But those who imagine that, by means of blood, and the smoke of sacrifices and burnt-offerings, they offer sacrifices [acceptable] to Him, and that by such honours they show Him respect, —these, by supposing that they can give anything to Him who stands in need of nothing, appear to me in no respect to differ from those who studiously confer the same honour on things destitute of sense, and which therefore are unable to enjoy such honours.

Chapter IV.—The other observances of the Jews.

But as to their scrupulosity concerning meats, and their superstition as respects the Sabbaths, and their boasting about circumcision, and their fancies about fasting and the new moons, which are utterly ridiculous and unworthy of notice,—I do not think that you require to learn anything from me. For, to accept some of those things which have been formed by God for the use of men as properly formed, and to reject others as useless and redundant,—how can this be lawful? And to speak falsely of God, as if He forbade us to do what is good on the Sabbath-days, —how is not this impious? And to glory in the circumcision of the flesh as a proof of election, and as if, on account of it, they were specially beloved by God,—how is it not a subject of ridicule? And as to their observing months and days, as if waiting upon the stars and the moon, and their distributing, according to their own tendencies, the appointments of God, and the vicissitudes of the seasons, some for festivities, and others for mourning,—who would deem this a part of divine worship, and not much rather a manifestation of folly? I suppose, then, you are sufficiently convinced that the Christians properly abstain from the vanity and error common [to both Jews and Gentiles], and from the busy-body spirit and vain boasting of the Jews; but you must not hope to learn the mystery of their peculiar mode of worshipping God from any mortal.

Chapter V.—The manners of the Christians.

For the Christians are distinguished from other men neither by country, nor language, nor the customs which they observe. For they neither inhabit cities of their own, nor employ a peculiar form of speech, nor lead a life which is marked out by any singularity. The course of conduct which they follow has not been devised by any speculation or deliberation of inquisitive men; nor do they, like some, proclaim themselves the advocates of any merely human doctrines. But, inhabiting Greek as well as barbarian cities, according as the lot of each of them has determined, and following the customs of the natives in respect to clothing, food, and the rest of their ordinary conduct, they display to us their wonderful and confessedly striking method of life. They dwell in their own countries, but simply as sojourners. As citizens, they share in all things with others, and yet endure all things as if foreigners. Every foreign land is to them as their native country, and every land of their birth as a land of strangers. They marry, as do all [others]; they beget children; but they do not destroy their offspring. They have a common table, but not a common bed. They are in the flesh, but they do not live after the flesh. They pass their days on earth, but they are citizens of heaven. They obey the prescribed laws, and at the same time surpass the laws by their lives. They love all men, and are persecuted by all. They are unknown and condemned; they are put to death, and restored to life. They are poor, yet make many rich; they are in lack of all things, and yet abound in all; they are dishonoured, and yet in their very dishonour are glorified. They are evil spoken of, and yet are justified; they are reviled, and bless; they are insulted, and repay the insult with honour; they do good, yet are punished as evil-doers. When punished, they rejoice as if quickened into life; they are assailed by the Jews as foreigners, and are persecuted by the Greeks; yet those who hate them are unable to assign any reason for their hatred.

.

Chapter VI.—The relation of Christians to the world.

To sum up all in one word—what the soul is in the body, that are Christians in the world. The soul is dispersed through all the members of the body, and Christians are scattered through all the cities of the world. The soul dwells in the body, yet is not of the body; and Christians dwell in the world, yet are not of the world. The invisible soul is guarded by the visible body, and Christians are known indeed to be in the world, but their godliness remains invisible. The flesh hates the soul, and wars against it, though itself suffering no injury, because it is prevented from enjoying pleasures; the world also hates the Christians, though in nowise injured, because they abjure pleasures. The soul loves the flesh that hates it, and [loves also] the members; Christians likewise love those that hate them. The soul is imprisoned in the body, yet preserves that very body; and Christians are confined in the world as in a prison, and yet they are the preservers of the world. The immortal soul dwells in a mortal tabernacle; and Christians dwell as sojourners in corruptible [bodies], looking for an incorruptible dwelling in the heavens. The soul, when but ill-provided with food and drink, becomes better; in like manner, the Christians, though subjected day by day to punishment, increase the more in number. God has assigned them this illustrious position, which it were unlawful for them to forsake.

Chapter VII.—The manifestation of Christ.

For, as I said, this was no mere earthly invention which was delivered to them, nor is it a mere human system of opinion, which they judge it right to preserve so carefully, nor has a dispensation of mere human mysteries been committed to them, but truly God Himself, who is almighty, the Creator of all things, and invisible, has sent from heaven, and placed among men, [Him who is] the truth, and the holy and incomprehensible Word, and has firmly established Him in their hearts. He did not, as one might have imagined, send to men any servant, or angel, or ruler, or any one of those who bear sway over earthly things, or one of those to whom the government of things in the heavens has been entrusted, but the very Creator and Fashioner of all things—by whom He made the heavens—by whom he enclosed the sea within its proper bounds—whose ordinances all the stars faithfully observe—from whom the sun has received the measure of his daily course to be ob- served— whom the moon obeys, being commanded to shine in the night, and whom the stars also obey, following the moon in her course; by whom all things have been arranged, and placed within their proper limits, and to whom all are subject—the heavens and the things that are therein, the earth and the things that are therein, the sea and the things that are therein—fire, air, and the abyss—the things which are in the heights, the things which are in the depths, and the things which lie between. This [messenger] He sent to them. Was it then, as one might conceive, for the purpose of exercising tyranny, or of inspiring fear and terror? By no means, but under the influence of clemency and meekness. As a king sends his son, who is also a king, so sent He Him; as God He sent Him; as to men He sent Him; as a Saviour He sent Him, and as seeking to persuade, not to compel us; for violence has no place in the character of God. As calling us He sent Him, not as vengefully pursuing us; as loving us He sent Him, not as judging us. For He will yet send Him to judge us, and who shall endure His appearing? ... Do you not see them exposed to wild beasts, that they may be persuaded to deny the Lord, and yet not overcome? Do you not see that the more of them are punished, the greater becomes the number of the rest? This does not seem to be the work of man: this is the power of God; these are the evidences of His manifestation.

Chapter VIII.—The miserable state of men before the coming of the Word.

For, who of men at all understood before His coming what God is? Do you accept of the vain and silly doctrines of those who are deemed trustworthy philosophers? of whom some said that fire was God, calling that God to which they themselves were by and by to come; and some water; and others some other of the elements formed by God. But if any one of these theories be worthy of approbation, every one of the rest of created things might also be declared to be God. But such declarations are simply the startling and erroneous utterances of deceivers; and no man has either seen Him, or made Him known, but He has revealed Himself. And He has manifested Himself through faith, to which alone it is given to behold God. For God, the Lord and Fashioner of all things, who made all things, and assigned them their several positions, proved Himself not merely a friend of mankind, but also long-suffering [in His dealings with them]. Yea, He was always of such a character, and still is, and will ever be, kind and good, and free from wrath, and true, and the only one who is [absolutely] good; and He formed in His mind a great and unspeakable conception, which He communicated to His Son alone. As long, then, as He held and preserved His own wise counsel in concealment, He appeared to neglect us, and to have no care over us. But after He revealed and laid open, through His beloved Son, the things which had been prepared from the beginning, He conferred every blessing all at once upon us, so that we should both share in His benefits, and see and be active [in His service]. Who of us would ever have expected these things? He was aware, then, of all things in His own mind, along with His Son, according to the relation subsisting between them.

Chapter IX.—Why the Son was sent so late.

As long then as the former time endured, He permitted us to be borne along by unruly impulses, being drawn away by the desire of pleasure and various lusts. This was not that He at all delighted in our sins, but that He simply endured them; nor that He approved the time of working iniquity which then was, but that He sought to form a mind conscious of righteousness, so that being convinced in that time of our unworthiness of attaining life through our own works, it should now, through the kindness of God, be vouchsafed to us; and having made it manifest that in ourselves we were unable to enter into the kingdom of God, we might through the power of God be made able. But when our wickedness had reached its height, and it had been clearly shown that its reward, punishment and death, was impending over us; and when the time had come which God had before appointed for manifesting His own kindness and power, how the one love of God, through exceeding regard for men, did not regard us with hatred, nor thrust us away, nor remember our iniquity against us, but showed great long-suffering, and bore with us, He Himself took on Him the burden of our iniquities, He gave His own Son as a ransom for us, the holy One for transgressors, the blameless One for the wicked, the righteous One for the unrighteous, the incorruptible One for the corruptible, the immortal One for them that are mortal. For what other thing was capable of covering our sins than His righteousness? By what other one was it possible that we, the wicked and ungodly, could be justified, than by the only Son of God? O sweet exchange! O unsearchable operation! O benefits surpassing all expectation! that the wickedness of many should be hid in a single righteous One, and that the righteousness of One should justify many transgressors! Having therefore convinced us in the former time that our nature was unable to attain to life, and having now revealed the Saviour who is able to save even those things which it was [formerly] impossible to save, by both these facts He desired to lead us to trust in His kindness, to esteem Him our Nourisher, Father, Teacher, Counsellor, Healer, our Wisdom, Light, Honour, Glory, Power, and Life, so that we should not be anxious concerning clothing and food.

Chapter X.—The blessings that will flow from faith.

If you also desire [to possess] this faith, you likewise shall receive first of all the knowledge of the Father. For God has loved mankind, on whose account He made the world, to whom He rendered subject all the things that are in it, to whom He gave reason and understanding, to whom alone He imparted the privilege of looking upwards to Himself, whom He formed after His own image, to whom He sent His only-begotten Son, to whom He has promised a kingdom in heaven, and will give it to those who have loved Him. And when you have attained this knowledge, with what joy do you think you will be filled? Or, how will you love Him who has first so loved you? And if you love Him, you will be an imitator of His kindness. And do not wonder that a man may become an imitator of God. He can, if he is willing. For it is not by ruling over his neighbours, or by seeking to hold the supremacy over those that are weaker, or by being rich, and showing violence towards those that are inferior, that happiness is found; nor can any one by these things become an imitator of God. But these things do not at all constitute His majesty. On the contrary he who takes upon himself the burden of his neighbour; he who, in whatsoever respect he may be superior, is ready to benefit another who is deficient; he who, whatsoever things he has received from God, by distributing these to the needy, becomes a god to those who receive [his bene- fits]: he is an imitator of God. Then thou shalt see, while still on earth, that God in the heavens rules over [the universe]; then thou shall begin to speak the mysteries of God; then shalt thou both love and admire those that suffer punishment because they will not deny God; then shall thou condemn the deceit and error of the world when thou shall know what it is to live truly in heaven, when thou shalt despise that which is here esteemed to be death, when thou shalt fear what is truly death, which is reserved for those who shall be condemned to the eternal fire, which shall afflict those even to the end that are committed to it. Then shalt thou admire those who for righteousness' sake endure the fire that is but for a moment, and shalt count them happy when thou shalt know [the nature of] that fire.

Chapter XI.—These things are worthy to be known and believed.

I do not speak of things strange to me, nor do I aim at anything inconsistent with right reason; but having been a disciple of the Apostles, I am become a teacher of the Gentiles. I minister the things delivered to me to those that are disciples worthy of the truth. For who that is rightly taught and begotten by the loving Word, would not seek to learn accurately the things which have been clearly shown by the Word to His disciples, to whom the Word being manifested has revealed them, speaking plainly [to them], not understood indeed by the unbelieving, but conversing with the disciples, who, being esteemed faithful by Him, acquired a knowledge of the mysteries of the Father? For which reason He sent the Word, that He might be manifested to the world; and He, being despised by the people [of the Jews], was, when preached by the Apostles, believed on by the Gentiles. This is He who was from the beginning, who appeared as if new, and was found old, and yet who is ever born afresh in the hearts of the saints. This is He who, being from everlasting, is to-day called the Son; through whom the Church is enriched, and grace, widely spread, increases in the saints, furnishing understanding, revealing mysteries, announcing times, rejoicing over the faithful, giving to those that seek, by whom the limits of faith are not broken through, nor the boundaries set by the fathers passed over. Then the fear of the law is chanted, and the grace of the prophets is known, and the faith of the gospels is established, and the tradition of the Apostles is preserved, and the grace of the Church exults; which grace if you grieve not, you shall know those things which the Word teaches, by whom He wills, and when He pleases. For whatever things we are moved to utter by the will of the Word commanding us, we communicate to you with pains, and from a love of the things that have been revealed to us.

Chapter XII.—The importance of knowledge to true spiritual life.

When you have read and carefully listened to these things, you shall know what God bestows on such as rightly love Him, being made [as ye are] a paradise of delight, presenting in yourselves a tree bearing all kinds of produce and flourishing well, being adorned with various fruits. For in this place the tree of knowledge and the tree of life have been planted; but it is not the tree of knowledge that destroys— it is disobedience that proves destructive. Nor truly are those words without significance which are written, how God from the beginning planted the tree of life in the midst of paradise, revealing through knowledge the way to life, and when those who were first formed did not use this [knowledge] properly, they were, through the fraud of the Serpent, stripped naked. For neither can life exist without knowledge, nor is knowledge secure without life. Wherefore both were planted close together. The Apostle, perceiving the force [of this conjunction], and blaming that knowledge which, without true doctrine, is admitted to influence life, declares, "Knowledge puffeth up, but love edifieth." For he who thinks he knows anything without true knowledge, and such as is witnessed to by life, knows nothing, but is deceived by the Serpent, as not loving life. But he who combines knowledge with fear, and seeks after life, plants in hope, looking for fruit. Let your heart be your wisdom; and let your life be true knowledge inwardly received. Bearing this tree and displaying its fruit, thou shalt always gather in those things which are desired by God, which the Serpent cannot reach, and to which deception does not approach; nor is Eve then corrupted, but is trusted as a virgin; and salvation is manifested, and the Apostles are filled with understanding, and the Passover of the Lord advances, and the choirs are gathered together, and are arranged in proper order, and the Word rejoices in teaching the saints,—by whom the Father is glorified: to whom be glory for ever. Amen.

Made in United States
North Haven, CT
26 April 2023

35930350R00017